Dear Mary Lou & Doug,

We pray your journey to Jerusalem will be a true pilgrimage of your souls. May you experience the love of God, the Presence of Jesus and the grace of the Holy Spirit.

We love you.

Suzanne and Mike

KNEELING IN
JERUSALEM

Other Large Print Books by Ann Weems
Published by Westminster/John Knox Press

Kneeling in Bethlehem

KNEELING IN JERUSALEM

ANN WEEMS

Westminster/John Knox Press
Louisville, Kentucky

"Lent" and "Put Away the Tinsel" were originally published in *Searching for Shalom* (Louisville, Ky.: Westminster/John Knox Press, 1991) and are used by permission.

Book design by Publishers' WorkGroup

Illustrations by Cecilia Amorocho

Cover design by Creative Publishing Services

First large print edition

Published by Westminster/John Knox Press
Louisville, Kentucky

This book is printed on acid-free paper that meets the American National Standards Institute Z39.48 standard. ∞

PRINTED IN THE UNITED STATES OF AMERICA
9 8 7 6 5 4 3 2 1

Library of Congress Cataloging-in-Publication Data

Weems, Ann
    Kneeling in Jerusalem / Ann Weems. — 1st large print ed.
        p.   cm.
    ISBN 0-664-25515-9 (pbk. : acid–free paper)

    1. Jesus Christ—Passion—Poetry.   2. Christian poetry, American.
3. Lent—Poetry.   4. Large type books.   I. Title.
[PS3573.E354K54   1993]
811' . 54—dc20   93-13217

To Heather,
pure in heart

CONTENTS

ON OUR WAY

THE HOLY IN THE ORDINARY

Holy is the time and holy is this place,
    and there are holy things that must be said.

Let us say to one another what our souls whisper . . .
    O Holy One, cast your tent among us;
    come into our ordinary lives and bless the living!

Forty days stretch before us,
    forty days of hungering after faithfulness,
        forty days of trying to understand the story,
and then, Holy Week . . .
O God, if every week were holy . . .

These forty days stretch before us,
    and those of us who believe
        yearn to feel Your presence,
        yearn to be Your people;
    and yet, the days fill with ordinary things
        with no time left
        for seeking the holy.

Spiritual contemplation is all right
    for those who have the time,
    but most of us have to make a living.

Most of us have to live in the real world
    where profanity splashes and blots out
        anything holy.

Where, O Holy One, can we find You in this unholy mess?

How, O God, can we find the holy in the ordinary?

LOOKING TOWARD JERUSALEM

The journey to Bethlehem
   was much more to my liking.
I am content kneeling here,
   where there's an aura of angels
and the ever-present procession
   of shepherds and of kings
who've come to kneel to the Newborn
   in whom we are newborn.

II

I want to linger here in Bethlehem
   in joy and celebration,
     knowing once I set my feet
      toward Jerusalem,
   the Child will grow,
     and I will be asked to follow.

III

The time of Light and Angels
   is drawing to a close.
Just when I've settled contentedly
   into the quiet wonder of Star and Child,
He bids me leave
   and follow.

How can I be expected to go back
   into darkness
after sitting mangerside,
   bathed in such Light?

IV

It's hard to get away
   this time of year;
I don't know how I'll manage.
It's not just the time . . .
   the conversation along the way
     turns from Birth to Death.
I'm not sure I can stand
   the stress and pain;
I have enough of those already.
Besides, I've found the lighting
   on the road to Jerusalem
     is very poor.
This time around, there is no Star . . .

V

The shepherds have left;
   they've returned to hillside
     and to sheep.

The Magi, too, have gone,
    having been warned in a dream,
as was Joseph,
    who packed up his family and fled.
If I stay in Bethlchem,
    I stay alone.
God has gone on
    toward Jerusalem.

FOR LOVE OF BETHLEHEM,
FOR FEAR OF JERUSALEM

Just when we were beginning
    to enjoy the play,
the stagehands came out
    and dismantled the manger.
From its wood,
    they built a cross.
What kind of a drama is this anyway?

The happy ending wasn't
    an ending after all,
    but just act I.

Before the play is over,
    most of the audience has left,
but the Director goes on,
    content with the remnant
to whom is promised
    a smashing finale.

Shall we, too, go home early—
    before we get stuck in the traffic?
We can always read
    what the critics have to say,
and if it's really good,
    we can be assured
    it will be repeated.

PUT AWAY THE TINSEL

When Lent comes,
    you have to put away the tinsel;
you have to take down your Christmas tree,
    and stand out in the open . . . vulnerable.
You either are or you aren't.
You either believe or you don't.
You either will or you won't.
And, O Lord, how we love the stable and the star!
When Lent comes the angels' voices
    begin their lamenting,
and we find ourselves in a courtyard
    where we must answer
whether we know him or not.

ASH WEDNESDAY

Ash Wednesday
  and we are on our way
  to Your Way.
O Lamb of God,
  have mercy upon us and
  keep us from all the smallness of our lives
  that would take precedence over
    kneeling in Jerusalem.

ASHES

Two nights ago I knelt and
   took the ashes from the fireplace.
It was some time before I saw evidence
   of the smudge of ash upon my face.
I washed it quickly away.

Last night I knelt and took the bread
   and dipped it in the cup,
and then I felt the cool smooth
   finger of ash upon my forehead,
ashes from last year's palms
   saved for this holy time.
I wondered if there might still be
   some remnant of Hosanna!
lingering in the ashes.

All evening long I wore the ash,
   that holy ash,
and when others saw the smudge,
   I wondered if they were inclined
to wipe it clean
   or to lean closer
in the hope of hearing
   some soft Hosanna!
burning still
   in ash
or heart . . .

LENT

Lent is a time to take the time
    to let the power of our faith story take hold of us,
a time to let the events
    get up and walk around in us,
a time to intensify
    our living unto Christ,
a time to hover over
    the thoughts of our hearts,
a time to place our feet in the streets of Jerusalem
    or to walk along the sea and listen to his word,
a time to touch his robe
    and feel the healing surge through us,
a time to ponder and a time to wonder . . .

Lent is a time to allow a fresh new taste of God!

THE WALK

Those of us who walk along this road
    do so reluctantly.
Lent is not our favorite time of year.

We'd rather be more active—
    planning and scurrying around.
All this is too contemplative to suit us.
Besides we don't know what to do
    with piousness and prayer.

Perhaps we're afraid to have time to think,
    for thoughts come unbidden.
Perhaps we're afraid to face our future
    knowing our past.
Give us the courage, O God,
    to hear your word
    and to read our living into it.
Give us the trust to know we're forgiven,
    and give us the faith
    to take up our lives and walk.

JOURNEY TO JERUSALEM

Our Grandfather's house
   was filled with death,
and we didn't want to feel it,
   so we stayed at home
      in snowfall and laughter.

She went alone
   and wept without us.

We're sorry, Mama,
   but it's not supposed
to snow in April,
   not in Tennessee.

ALONG
THE WAY

THE WAY

The way to Jerusalem
   looks suspiciously like Highway 40,
and the pilgrims
   look suspiciously like you and me.
I expected the road to Jerusalem
   to be crowded with holy people . . .
clerics and saints . . .
   people who have kindness wrinkled in their faces
and comfort lingering in their voices,
   but this is more like rush hour . . .
horns blowing, people pushing, voices cursing. . . .
   This is not what I envisioned!

O God, I've only begun and already
   I feel I've lost my way.
Surely this is not the road
   and surely these
are not the ones
   to travel with me.
This Lenten journey calls for
   holy retreat,
for reflection
   and repentance.

Instead of holiness
   the highway is crammed

with the cacophony
    of chaos.
Is there no back road
    to Jerusalem?
No quiet path
    where angels tend
to weary travelers?
    No sanctuary
from the noise of the world?
    Just this?
Can this hectic highway
    be the highway to heaven?

BELONGING

Full communion in the church
   doesn't mean what it used to.
Even those who belong don't belong
   if they don't have the rights
     and privileges of the others.
The list of nonbelonging belongers is long.
If you're included in the list
   (which means you're excluded),
     you know it,
       even though you've been assured
        that the belonging believers
          have compassion for your plight.

Fortunately, you know from
   the scriptures and confessions
     that you belong where it counts.
Your options include
   turning the other check
     and assuring the belonging believers
       that you have compassion for their plight.
Blessed are the poor in privilege,
   for they belong to God.

THE DISCIPLES

Hurting, they came to him.
Healed, they followed him.
Grateful, they gave to him
    what they had and what they were.
Blessed, they became a blessing
    and went out to all the world
        in his name.

Those who are hurt
        and healed
        grateful
        and blessed
still move among us
        in his name.

THE VISIT

I went to visit her,
but dreaded seeing
her body cancer-filled.
What I saw upon her bed
was a small bag of yellowed skin
full of bones.
She faced the window
away from the door I entered,
and I heard her whisper
this prayer:
"Thank you, God;
I had a nice time."

WALKING RAINBOWS

A rainbow is not just a symphony of colors
   sent to calm the storm in our souls;
     it is a talk with God,
   a mysterious, miraculous conversation with God,
     heart to heart,
the very heart of God saying to our hearts:
   "I remember I am your God.
     Be my walking rainbows,
       so that the whole world
         will know to whom you belong,
   for I am the God who keeps promises,
     and I have not forgotten our covenant."
This is the hope of the church:
   that God keeps promises.
The mission of the church is to
   walk among the suffering and give,
     for we are covenant keepers,
       walking rainbows,
   bringing the hope of the good news to the poor.

MEMORY

We sit in memory,
   chocolate on our faces,
receiving
   love in an Easter basket
        and
   hope in a Red Letter Testament.

For that time,
   it was more than enough.

CHURCHGOERS

The man sat down and said,
   "This pew is too hard!"
The woman sat down and said,
   "This pew is too soft!"
The child sat down and said,
   "This pew is just right!"
Some get in the habit of denigrating
   when it's just as easy
to get in the habit of celebrating.

GOD'S GRAFFITI

We've splashed our rules
all over the sanctuary walls . . .
so many rules we don't have time
   for dancing . . .
our graffiti
   defiling the house of God.
God's graffiti is different:
   God writes LOVE
      upon our hearts.
Some night, let's sneak in the sanctuary
   and paint over the rules
   and write God's graffiti
all over the walls . . .
   LOVE LOVE LOVE LOVE

A LISTENING

Going through Lent
    is a listening.
When we listen
    to the word,
we hear
    where we are so
blatantly
    unliving.
If we listen to the word,
    and hallow it
into our lives,
    we hear
how we can so
    abundantly
live again.

BEHOLD YOUR MOTHER

It is not much the mailman brings
   to wrinkled women isolated
      in unfamiliar cubicles
they are asked to call home.

It is not much the women see
   within a day's expanse . . .
      a nurse or two, smiling or brusque.
It's not their mother
   or their daughter
      or anybody they ever saw
before they saw this building
   that they never saw before
they came to live here.

It is not much they've come to expect,
   these women born with hope in their veins
      and feet that learned to dance.
They sit now, staring at nothing in particular,
   no longer even vaguely thinking
that the footsteps in the hall
   will stop at their door.

Lord, are we our mothers' keepers?

HAVE MERCY ON US

O God, from whose eyes the measure of our faith is not hidden, wrench from us now all religiosity, all rules and regulations of our scheduled selves that separate us from your Holy Spirit.

O God, who calls each of us by name to be the church, give us love enough to make a difference, give us vision enough to follow, give us endurance enough to hold steadfast in the face of the unholy.

O God, who claims us as disciples, bless us now and touch us with your holiness that we might have commitment enough to be good news to the poor.

O God of the bruised, we pray for healing. Comfort those who cry in dark corners: the lonely, the strangers, the weary, the fearful, the disappointed, the anxious, the depressed, the forsaken, the dispirited, the grieving, and those who lie in sickness and in pain.

O God who wept over Jerusalem, open our eyes to those around us who scream in silence the depth of their despair.

O God of compassion, heal our hard hearts to tenderness.

O God of the oppressed, fire us with justice that we might proclaim liberty to the captives.

O God who gave us the rainbow and parted the Red Sea, we dare to pray for miracles for the powerless.

O God of the hungry, we pray for those who have not bread. Remove, O God, the bondage of hunger by removing our shackles so that we might share our bread.

O God of the homeless, we pray for those who have no land. We pray that you will open the doors of our hearts and let your wandering people in.

O God of the captives, have mercy on those who must live out their lives enslaved to someone else because of race or politics or economics or faith. Loose our bonds that we might risk our own securities on their behalf.

O God of peace, give peace to our hearts and to our nation and to our world.

O Lamb of God, have mercy upon us!

FORGIVE, O HOLY ONE

Stressed and anxious,
the people come
to be comforted
and are put in committee.
Forgive, O Holy One,
our weariness
with your world
and with your word.

THE LAST SHALL BE FIRST

Along the way the pilgrims heard
    that a group of people
had set out for Jerusalem
    without a map.
Since each of us owned
    our own map
and read it daily
    and even then
had difficulty knowing
    which way to turn,
we were amazed
    that they would set out
on their own . . .
    amazed and alarmed.
Many a day we had
    prayed and consulted
over choices
    in the road.
This news presented
    a greater dilemma:
Which of us would go
    in the rescue party?
Whoever went would
    most certainly
not get to Jerusalem
    on time.

Distraught,
  we prayed.
Then it was we realized
  that the ones who went
in search of the lost
  would be the first
to arrive in Jerusalem.

CAREFUL CONSIDERATION

Certain in-charge church people
    expound upon the finer points of doctrine
while the disenfranchised await the verdict.

Meanwhile the holy fools rush in
    and touch the outcasts,
creating Good News once again.

WE PRAY THIS DAY

O God, we pray this day:
for all who have a song they cannot sing,
for all who have a burden they cannot bear,
for all who live in chains they cannot break,
for all who wander homeless and cannot return,
for those who are sick and for those who tend them,
for those who wait for loved ones
   and wait in vain,
for those who live in hunger
   and for those who will not share their bread,
for those who are misunderstood
   and for those who misunderstand,
for those who are captives and for those who are captors,
for those whose words of love are locked within their hearts
   and for those who yearn to hear those words.

Have mercy upon these, O God.
Have mercy upon us all.

STEWARDSHIP

The pew preached to the pulpit,
  all the while clutching its checkbook.
The pulpit hung its head,
  and tried to quiet its conscience
with these considerations:
    If the greatest givers are offended,
      mission will go unfunded.
    If the boat is rocked,
      it is the poor who will be drowned.
The conscience spoke back:
    Answer me this one:
      Do we owe our soul to the Company Church?

THE WAY TO JERUSALEM
IS CLUTTERED

The way to Jerusalem
   is cluttered
with bits and pieces of our lives
   that fly up and cry out,
wounding us as we try
   to keep upon this path
that leads to Life.

Why didn't somebody tell us
   that it would be so hard?

In the midst of the clutter,
   the children laugh
     and run after stars.
Those of us who are wise
   will follow,
for the children will be the first
   to kneel in Jerusalem.

SHAKING THE DUST
FROM OFF THEIR FEET

He asked them point blank
   why they didn't stop by anymore.
At first they responded politely
   that they'd been awfully busy,
but would certainly be calling
   one of these days real soon.
Pressed, they spewed it out:
   Despite their efforts
   to care and to comfort,
   he refused to see
   any stars in his dark skies.
The community could no longer stay
   waiting for his eyes to see,
but had to continue, as always,
   in search of Light.
You know, they said,
   where you can find us.

THE NUMBERS GAME

Number 1: On Forgiving Each Other

70 times 7 . . .
    a bit excessive, don't you think?
We're supposed to forgive each other 70 times 7.
Let's see: 70 times 7 is 490,
    but who's counting?
490 for you and for him and for her and for them. . . .
We'd need accountants!
How could we ever keep track?
Or is that the point?

Number 2: The Pastor's Priorities

99 percent of the congregation complains
    (or at least frowns)
because the pastor is out of the office
    (so much of the time).

Where, pray tell, is he?

    Finding one lost sheep.

99 percent of the congregation complains.
Meanwhile, in heaven,
    the angels are rejoicing.

Number 3: 30 Pieces of Silver

30 pieces of silver
   pass down the centuries
      from hand to hand
   burning into hearts
      too cold
   to have the eyes to see.

Number 4: Wherever 2 or 3

2 or 3 . . .
It doesn't even have to be
   Sunday morning.
It doesn't have to be
   in the sanctuary.
We don't have to have
   flowers
or even music—
   not even the clergy.
Just 2 or 3 gathering in his name . . .
   and the Crucified and Risen One
      will be here with us.

WINDING DOWN

We run around the world and church
   like wound-up toys,
looking for a way to get to Easter
   without reading the instructions.
When we wind down,
   we lie on the floor
on our faces,
   unable to move.
Perhaps, in the still and the silence,
   God will give us the courage
to see our souls
   and give us the chance
once more
   to choose Life:
faith, rather than frenzy.

THE CHILDREN'S SERMON

When the time came
   for the children's sermon,
the congregation enjoyed
   the flurry of small bodies,
popping up here and there,
   racing to the front
of the sanctuary
   which, like the children,
was Easter-clad.
One small child,
   bottle in hand,
went down the aisle
   past the Communion table
to the steps in front of the pulpit,
   and sat with the others.
The minister greeted them and
   began by asking them
to hold out both their hands.
Not wanting to be left out,
   the child with the bottle
placed it on the table,
   the table that had been
properly prepared
   for Holy Communion.
Whether the congregation
   grimaced or grinned,

I cannot say,
    but some report to have heard
an extravaganza of bells
    that Easter Sunday,
when a plastic bottle,
    filled with the nourishment of life
        for this small child,
stood beside silver cup and plate
        filled with the nourishment of life
        for the souls of all present.
Of such is the kingdom of heaven. . . .

BUNNY AND BASKET

Bunny and basket are under attack.
The TV evangelist, shaking his fist,
   is preaching against
     the Easter bunny.
This time it's serious:
   for Easter dinner
     he's serving rabbit to the poor.
The question I have is this:
   Does bunny bashing
     lead people to love the Lamb?

HALLOWED

I could live in the prayer's beginning
HALLOWED HALLOWED HALLOWED
encircled in the symphony of a holy choir
   whose singing has no end,
but all too swiftly
   I am beyond that
and asking:
   GIVE GIVE GIVE
and more than daily bread.
Where do the words come from?
How does my voice insinuate itself
   into his prayer?
O Jesus, Jesus, Jesus,
   hold my hand . . .

COUNTING THE COST

The end begins
  with a woman
    who poured perfume
    upon his head.
She poured it lavishly,
  without counting the cost.
The disciples were angry;
  the perfume could have been
     sold
  and the money
    given
  to the poor.
Where have I heard that tune before?

Oh, what trouble we have with gifts and giving!
You want to tell me
  how much and when and to whom
and I want to tell you
  my way of giving is better than yours.
What Jesus told the disciples and us
     is:
  An extravagance of the heart
    is a fine and beautiful thing.

Why is it that this one is so hard for us?

IDOLATRY

The church doesn't want
   to talk about idols;
we never have.
Jeremiah knew that
   and so did Paul.
They were in trouble
   with the good church folk
who didn't want to think about
   smashing their idols.
We're no different.

The church today is
   swollen with idols
to whom we bring alms.
We're crowded with gods,
   too many to name,
but in spite of our protests,
   we know where we bow.
If budget making becomes
   more important than covenant keeping,
we're bowing to the wrong god.
If committee work takes precedence
   over worship,
we're bowing to the wrong god.

Idols?
    The church is cluttered.
If the sky falls,
    perhaps we'll fall, too . . .
on our knees.
From our knees, we can see
    to rise again
in that newness Paul
    wrote about.

If we take Jeremiah's advice
    to remember
who we are
    and to Whom we belong,
we'll have a chance
    at smashing our idols
and getting on with
    the Good News story.

COME UNTO ME

When the journey gets too hard,
when we feel depleted,
when our compassion
   turns to complaining,
when our efforts toward
   justice and mercy
   seem to get us nowhere,
it's time to remember
   the humility part—
that it is God who has made us
   and not we ourselves;
that the saving of the world
   or even one part of it
     is not on our shoulders.
It is then we can come unto him,
   and he will give us rest.
With rest we'll remember
   what it is we are about.

HEAVENLY NIGHTMARE

It is my recurring nightmare
   that heaven will be organized,
that some Martha will get there
   before I do and will be happily
buzzing about
   straightening clouds,
   ironing angels' gowns,
   starching wing tips,
   buffing stars,
and getting ready for the
   big hymn sing in the sky.
The nightmare is over
   before anyone calls a meeting
and asks me to take minutes.
   I'm filled with eternal gratitude. . . .

EVEN NOW

She stands
   beneath his dying
and will not be persuaded to leave,
   despite the urgings of the others.
They huddle against her
   in an effort to hold her
against the pain,
   but she stands erect,
unleaning,
   her eyes upon his face.
From the hillside
   the sounds of weeping and wailing
hang heavy in the air,
   but she who held him
in a stable in Bethlehem
   stands silent
beneath his cross in Jerusalem,
   her heart pondering still,
   her soul magnifying the Lord,
   her spirit praising God,
knowing even now
   that she is blessed among women.

WALKING THROUGH FRIDAY

The gift of myrrh
   went from manger to cross.
Mary and Joseph said
   thank you to the kings,
but Jesus, on the cross,
   when offered wine with myrrh,
   said no.
There are times when we, too,
   must go heartlong into our pain,
knowing it's the only way
   we will get to Easter living.

WITNESS

"I am a Christian," one once said to me.
  He said it loudly.
I watched and said:
"I shall not be."

OUR DREAMS

Sometimes the pages won't turn
    in our book of dreams,
and we are left clinging to a life
    we never lived . . .
        just wanted to.
Stuck in the stark reality
    of unlived dreams,
we sniffle and tread water,
    or we go in search
        of the Holy One
who will wipe the tears
    from our eyes
and offer to us
    the only dream
        that lives.

ONE OUT OF TEN

There was one
who said "Thank you!"
One out of ten . . .
and Jesus asked:
What happened
to the other nine?
Blessings on that one
who taught us
how to worship.

TO WORSHIP

When the people of God
gather for worship,
the whole earth trembles
and the angels sing.

THANK YOU

Thank you,
Jesus God Spirit
who is Holy
on us.

Anointing us
with amazing love
you dug a dwelling place
and settled
tenaciously
forever amen within us.

Thank you,
Jesus God Spirit
who is Holy
on us
for your incredible grace.

MIRACLE

There's been a call for a miracle,
    but Jesus says no:
The only miracle going is Jonah's.
Jonah and Jesus in fish and earth,
    buried,
        then catapulted
            to new life.
You want a miracle?
The miracle is in believing.
Ask the Queen of Sheba
or the people of Ninevah.
Then go your way and live forever.

A GATE CALLED TRUTH

Just outside Jerusalem
   we came to a gate called Truth.
We called to the gatekeeper
   to let us in.
"The latch is not on," he replied.
"Anyone who will can enter."
We went closer,
   but seeing how great
   and how heavy was the gate,
we looked for a way around.
   There must be a way around.

THE WAY TO JERUSALEM

The pilgrims trudge
  toward the death of God.
Only with bowed heads and closed eyes
  will they be able to see
    the way to Jerusalem.

HOLY WEEK

HOLY WEEK

Holy is the week . . .
Holy, consecrated, belonging to God . . .
We move from hosannas to horror
   with the predictable ease
      of those who know not what they do.
Our hosannas sung,
  our palms waved,
let us go with passion into this week.
It is a time to curse fig trees that do not yield fruit.
It is a time to cleanse our temples of any blasphemy.
It is a time to greet Jesus as the Lord's Anointed One,
   to lavishly break our alabaster
   and pour perfume out for him
     without counting the cost.
It is a time for preparation . . .
The time to give thanks and break bread is upon us.
The time to give thanks and drink of the cup is imminent.
Eat, drink, remember:
On this night of nights, each one must ask,
  as we dip our bread in the wine,
    "Is it I?"
And on that darkest of days, each of us must stand
  beneath the tree
and watch the dying
  if we are to be there
when the stone is rolled away.

The only road to Easter morning
   is through the unrelenting shadows of that Friday.
Only then will the alleluias be sung;
   only then will the dancing begin.

THE FEAR AND FEEDING OF THE SHEEP

We have nothing against Jerusalem;
    in fact, it's the place to be
        on a sunny Easter morning.
It's Golgotha that we fear;
    and yet, we've been to church enough
        to know that the way to Jerusalem
            leads through Good Friday.
Keeping covenant
    means keeping covenant under a cross
        as well as by an empty garden tomb.
What we'd like to do, of course,
    is wave palms and shout Hosanna
        and then rest up
            for the Hallelujah Chorus.
We dismiss the others as religious fanatics,
    who wallow in the woe of Holy Week!
O Lamb of God, Lamb of God, Lamb of God,
    feed us!

BETWEEN PARADES

We're good at planning!
Give us a task force
   and a project
      and we're off and running!
No trouble at all!
    Going to the village and finding the colt,
       even negotiating with the owners
         is right down our alley.
And how we love a parade!
In a frenzy of celebration
   we gladly focus on Jesus
      and generously throw our coats
        and palms in his path.
And we can shout praise
   loudly enough
      to make the Pharisees complain.
It's all so good!

It's between parades that
   we don't do so well.
From Sunday to Sunday
   we forget our hosannas.
Between parades
   the stones will have to shout
      because we don't.

JESUS WEEPING OVER JERUSALEM

There is but one face
   whose holy eyes
won't turn away,
   but focus on us
and weep . . .

Jesus, you!
   like a mother hen
yearning to gather us to you,
   but we would not . . .
for we have killed the prophets
   and stoned the messengers.

Now abandoned and empty,
   the stones of the temple
waiting to fall
   around our ankles,
we still do not come
   to you,
and, even now,
   you weep.

HOLY COMMUNION

Eat. Drink. Remember
   who I am.

Eat. Drink. Remember
   who I am
   so you can remember
   who you are.

Eat. Drink. Remember
   who I am
   so you can remember
   who you are
   and tell the others.

Eat. Drink. Remember
   who I am
   so you can remember
   who you are
   and tell the others
   so that all
   God's people
   can live
   in communion . . .
   in holy communion.

EASTER STREET

The clapping is hollow,
    synchronized and Muzak.
We simply find ourselves
    celebrating celebration,
dragging our feet
    in the wildwood
instead of running
    into the street.
We want our Life from Birth.
Instead we get Life from Death
        emptied from a tomb
        out of a garden
        into the street . . .
When will we learn
    that the music
will go undanced
    in the wildwood?
The only living is on Easter Street.

THE COURTYARD SCENE

Over and over again
   we sit in our courtyards,
our mouths speaking what our hearts are full of . . .
   WE DO NOT KNOW HIM.
DONOTDONOTDONOT
KNOWHIMKNOWHIMKNOWHIM echoes loudly
      emphatically
   filling time and space
      heaven and earth;
and yet
   the saddest part is
when the cock crows
   we don't have the ears to hear
TOHEARTOHEARTOHEAR.
At least Peter had the ears to hear
   and the heart to weep.

THE CHURCH

Screaming souls upon the shatterable Rock
nightmare.
In darkness we await the crow of the cock.

FRIDAY

The sky peels back to purple
   and thunder slaps the thighs of heaven,
and all the tears of those who grieve
   fly up to clouds and are released
and drench the earth.
The ones who see and hear
     know
   that all is lost.
The only One named Savior
     died
   upon a cross.
The ones who believed and loved
   huddle together
     stunned.
All night long
   the angels weep.

SOUVENIRS

When we entered Jerusalem,
   stars were handed out
      as souvenirs of
         our pilgrimage.
We tucked them
   next to our hearts
     and continued
        on our journey.
When we got to Friday
   in and in and in
     the nails were
        driven.
        In
     the terror of the thunder and
   the uncontrollable sobbing,
we dropped our stars.
Beneath the cross
   the ground is strewn
     with broken stars
        and kneeling pilgrims,

godforsaken.

IT IS FINISHED

The pilgrims sit on the
   steps of death.
Undanced,
   the music ends.
Only the children remember
   that tomorrow's stars
     are not yet out.

FAIR IS FAIR

We still don't like
   the way it was done.
The whole idea of a sacrificial Lamb
   is not to our liking.
What's fair is fair,
   and there was no justice here.
The Innocent One
The Righteous One
The Holy One
   put to death
because the ones in charge of politics
   wanted to hold onto their crowns
and the ones in charge of religion
   wanted to hold onto the keys to the church.
How could they do it????!!!!

NO DANCES

There are no dances for dark days.
There is no music to bellow the pain.
The best we can do is to remain
    still and silent
and try to remember the face of God . . .

    and how to kneel

    and how to pray.

SATURDAY SILENCE

The shadows shift and fly.
The
  whole
    long
      day
the air trembles,
  thick with silence,
until, finally,
  the footsteps are heard,
and the noise
  of the voice of God
    is upon us.
The Holy One
  is not afraid
    to walk
      on unholy ground.
The Holy Work is done,
  and the world awaits
    the dawn of Life.

THE STORY AND THE CHILD

The child comes,
   and we dye eggs
and make a cake
   and decorate.
"Why are we doing this?"
   he asks.
"Because," I answer,
   "Life is about to happen,
and on Sunday morning
   we'll catch stars."
He looks at me,
   quizzically at first,
and then grins.
It's then I ask him
   to tell me the story.
The only way he'll learn
   is to tell it himself.
The only way we'll learn
   is to tell it again . . .
and again . . .
   to the child.

THE VIGIL

The ham is cooked.
The apple float is made
    (just like my grandmother's),
and now I'll fill the baskets
and then to sleep,
but first I'll pray that
through the dark and silence
Easter morn will come.
I know too well
the sin
of taking things
for granted
and how adept we are
at extricating
holiness
from holy days.
Please, O God,
once more
forgive.

AMAZED

The people who heard Jesus
    were repeatedly amazed.
Are we today so sophisticated
    that we are immune to
        amazement?
Can we know that he was
    crucified,
Goodness and Compassion
    and Love
nailed upon the tree,
    and go about our business
        of preparing Easter dinner?
Can we know that he arose
    from the dead
    and walked the earth
    and ate and spoke
    with his followers
and sit unamazed in the pew
    as though we cannot hear
        the WORD OF GOD?
O God of Jesus the Christ,
    the amazing thing
is our lack of amazement
    in the face of your
        AMAZING AMEN!

TOURING JERUSALEM

The pilgrims come for
   prayers and photographs.
All the sacred spots are on the slides.
He may have stood here;
he may have walked there.
He was buried here
   or was it there?
The tomb of the Lamb of God
   is a tourist attraction.
The angels continue their lamenting.

ROOM IN THE HEART

Death abides not
    on a hill called Golgotha,
but in every heart that makes room.

Life abides not
    outside a garden tomb in Jerusalem,
but in every heart that makes room.

LOST AND FOUND

As we approached Jerusalem
   the crowd stood at the gate
and cried in tear-choked voice:
"We are lost
   in his death."

Upon the hill
   the angels sang:
"We are found
   in his rising."

EASTER

EASTER

Just when I thought
   there would be no more light
     in the Jerusalem sky,
the Bright and Morning Star
   appeared
     and the darkness has not overcome it.

THE TIME FOR KNEELING

The Lamb has been slain,
   and the sheep have scattered.
Now is the time for kneeling,
   the time for believers
to kneel and call upon his name,
   to kneel
     and to rise again:
the community of the resurrection.

IN SEARCH OF NEW RESURRECTIONS

We in the church are in danger
   of becoming a tearless people,
unable to rage even in a starless abyss.
We have imitated a smiling society,
   glossing over the hurt, the oppression,
   the peacelessness on earth,
or we have become caustic
   and cynical and despairing,
insisting on looking the other way
   as our church members crawl to the altar,
the scraps of their lives in their arms.

We were created for covenant keeping
   and yet, we are in danger
of becoming a blindhearted people,
   buying into the system,
placing our hope with kings and corporations.
Have we not seen?
Have we not heard?

We persist in clinging
   to the way things are,
or eagerly placing our faith
   in the newest religious fad,
     the latest book on how-to Christianity
      (in ten easy steps),

or the current slogans
    presented as though they were
        the Word of God.
We are programming and papering ourselves
    into perpetuity,
and rationalizing and excusing
    our immorality.
We spend our energy in complaining,
    gloomily forecasting our future together.
We panic for positions
    in employment and committee,
with each special interest group
    vying for first place in the kingdom.
Perhaps it's time for remembering
    that Jesus stood in the Jordan
        to be baptized with the others,
long ago casting his lot,
    not with the good church people,
        but with the poor
wherever that poverty might emerge.
His name is Emmanuel,
    and yet, individually and corporately,
        we have named him "GOD-WITH-ME."
Have we not seen?
Have we not heard?

In the light of the cross,
    the alternative is anything but hopelessness.
On the contrary!
There is every scriptural indication
    that we are called to change
        who we are into the kingdom of God.
Where change is possible,
    new resurrections loom!

EASTER MORNING

The stirring wildness of God
    calls brittle bones to leaping
and stone hearts to soaring.
Old women dance among the stars.

AND THE GLORY

The silence breaks into morning.
That One Star lights the world.
The lily springs to life and
   not even Solomon . . .

Let it begin with singing
   and never end!
Oh, angels, quit your lamenting!
Oh, pilgrims,
   upon your knees in tearful prayer,
     rise up
       and take your hearts
       and run!
We who were no people
   are named anew
     God's people,
for he who was no more
   is forevermore.